T0304985

CORNER SHOP COCKTAILS

ONE-STOP RECIPES
FOR QUICK & EASY DRINKS

Olive Martin

hamlyn

CONTENTS

INTRODUCTION

Nothing beats a cocktail at the end of a long day. But what if you haven't got the right ingredients to hand? What if you get home and your drinks cabinet suddenly looks a bit barren, and the limes in the fridge have gone mouldy? Fear not. Everything you need to put together a knockout cocktail can be found in your local corner shop, convenience store or bodega, and *Corner Shop Cocktails* is here to show you how.

First of all, forget what the cocktail purists tell you – with a bit of ingenuity, most classic cocktails can be created with readily available ingredients. Some of them are so simple that they only need two universal components. In the case of the Gimlet (see page 72), an aperitif straight from the Golden Age of cocktails, that means gin and lime cordial. Others can be recreated

with clever corner-shop tweaks, like swapping the Worcestershire sauce in a Bloody Mary (see page 23) for whatever chilli sauce you can find, or using strawberry jam for fruity sweetness in a Berry Margarita (see page 107). You might end up with something slightly different, but it will still be delicious. After all, professional mixologists have been using what's available to them to create new cocktails since the 1920s, when bartenders took the sting out of Prohibition liqueur by mixing it with more palatable flavours.

In order to swap different ingredients successfully, you need to consider the balance of the original cocktail. Think of sweetness and acidity as the salt and pepper of cocktail making: as with seasoning a dish, using these two things judiciously is the secret to a delicious drink. If you're using something sweeter than the original ingredient as a substitute, you may need an extra dash of lemon juice to correct the balance. Taste as you go, and don't be afraid to experiment. Take a look at the Ingredient Swaps section (see page 10) for more guidance on substitutions.

You don't need fancy kit either. If you don't have a cocktail shaker, you can use any receptacle – ideally made of glass, stainless steel or sturdy plastic – with a tight-fitting lid, along with a sieve or tea strainer. Turn to the Cocktail Hacks section (see page 6) for a list of handy shortcuts. Although classic cocktail recipes call for specific glasses such as rocks, highball or martini glasses, it really doesn't matter if you don't have the 'right' glass — just use one you like. A special glass of any kind will enhance the experience (see page 14).

Finally, remember that making a great cocktail isn't just about the ingredients. It's about preparing your drink carefully, making sure it's ice-cold (ice is the only

absolute must-have for cocktails, and your corner shop will likely provide that, too) and getting out your very best glasses. If you have time, chill your glasses and ingredients in the freezer in advance. If you don't, use the Cocktail Hacks for a shortcut (see page 6).

If you're generous with the ice, thoughtful with your decorations and take your time preparing the drink, no one will know you're serving them a corner-shop special. With this book as your guide, you can create the sense of occasion that a cocktail brings with whatever you have to hand.

COCKTAIL HACKS

No cocktail shaker?
Use a jam jar

If you don't have a cocktail shaker, any receptacle with a tight-fitting lid that doesn't leak, such as a clean jar or good-quality plastic container, will work fine.

Let your sieve
take the strain

Many cocktail shakers have a built-in strainer, but if you are using a jar with a lid, then use a small sieve or tea strainer to strain your cocktail into the glass.

Get out the
measuring spoons

If you don't have a cocktail jigger (a V-shaped stainless-steel measure that holds 25 ml/1 fl oz on one side and 50 ml/2 fl oz on the other), use measuring spoons or a small measuring jug.

If using measuring spoons:
One measure (25 ml/1 fl oz) =
1 tablespoon plus 2 teaspoons
Two measures (50 ml/2 fl oz) =
3 tablespoons plus 1 teaspoon

Be inventive
with decorations

If you don't have the decoration called
for in the recipe, be open to using
something else. A thin slice of apple
among ice cubes looks great; if you
don't have lemon, use an orange or
a lime; consider whether a celery leaf,
olive or herb might do the trick. A stash
of frozen fruit, such as cherries, comes
in handy too. You might even hit upon
a stellar new flavour combination! For
any drink served in a short tumbler with
ice, a short straw or cocktail stirrer will
bring a bit of flair.

Chill your glasses
in a flash

Pre-chilling your cocktail glasses
really does make a difference – when
a drink is served ice-cold it's much
more refreshing. Ideally, you'd put the
glasses in the fridge or freezer for an
hour before serving, but, if you haven't
done that, you can wrap the glasses
in wet tea towel and put them in the
coldest part of the freezer (usually at
the back, near the fan). They will be
very cold within a few minutes.

Use a rolling pin as a muddler

Professional bartenders use a muddler (a metal or wooden stick a bit like a pestle, with a jagged end) to crush ingredients such as citrus wedges, sugar or fresh herbs in the bottom of the shaker or glass to release their flavours. If you don't have one, the rounded end of a rolling pin will do just as well. Make sure you are using a robust glass with a base that can withstand a bit of pressure.

Make your own cracked or crushed ice

To make your own cracked ice, wrap ice cubes in a clean tea towel, place them on a sturdy surface and bash them with a wooden rolling pin until they've cracked into large chunks. For crushed ice, keep bashing until the ice has broken into 1–2 cm (½–1 inch) sized pieces. Crack or crush your ice just before you need it, as it will melt quickly.

No bar spoon?
Use a chopstick

Bartenders use long, fancy spoons for
stirring long drinks or for 'floating' layers
of ingredients on top of one another.
But a chopstick or a long straw can work
just as well as a stirrer, and any metal
spoon can be used for floating liquids
(see pages 43, 89 and 125).

Don't forget the cocktail
'furniture'

Adding a finishing touch turns an
ordinary drink into a fancy cocktail.
Coasters, stirrers, cocktail sticks and
straws – even cocktail umbrellas for
tropical-style cocktails like a Piña Colada
(see page 47) – show that care has been
taken in the preparation of the drink,
and therefore enhances the experience
of drinking it. If you are, or suspect you
may become, a cocktail enthusiast, it's
well worth building up a collection.

INGREDIENT SWAPS

Soda water

Soda water is carbonated water with a tiny amount of mineral salt (usually sodium bicarbonate), which gives it a slightly alkaline flavour. You can use ordinary carbonated mineral water instead. In some gin-based cocktails, tonic water might do as a substitute, but its distinctive flavour doesn't work in all cases.

Cointreau, Grand Marnier and triple sec

Cointreau is an orange liqueur used in many cocktails and can be found in most corner shops. It's a type of triple sec, a clear, sweet, orange-flavoured liqueur that originates from France. Many brands are available, and any type of triple sec can be used when a recipe calls for Cointreau. Curaçao is a similar liqueur that comes from the Caribbean island of the same name and is made from bitter oranges, most famously in the form of bright-hued blue Curaçao.

Grand Marnier is a brown, brandy-based orange liqueur with a richer, toastier, more complex flavour. Triple sec (including Cointreau) and Grand Marnier can be substituted for one another – there is a slight difference in taste and colour, but if you embrace the variation the cocktail will be just as good.

 ## Lemons and limes

 ## Sugar syrup

Although there are differences in flavour, lemons and limes can be substituted for one another in cocktails, especially when used as a decoration. In many cases, pink grapefruit is a better substitute than lemon for the slightly more aromatic flavour of lime. Freshly squeezed juice is always preferable, but bottled lemon or lime juice can be used at a push, if only a small amount is called for in the recipe. For very simple cocktails that rely on citrus juice, such as a Tom Collins (see page 73), only freshly squeezed will do.

This is used to sweeten many cocktails because it blends into a cold drink faster than ordinary sugar, and it gives the cocktail body. It is available ready-made, but it's easy to make your own. Put 4 tablespoons granulated sugar and 4 tablespoons water into a small saucepan and bring slowly to the boil, stirring to dissolve the sugar. Boil without stirring for 1–2 minutes, then leave to cool. Store in a sterilized bottle in the refrigerator for up to 2 months.

If you don't want (or have time) to make your own, you can use any light-flavoured syrup such as agave or carob syrup, or runny honey.

Coconut milk and cream

Grenadine

When a cocktail recipe calls for coconut milk, the first choice would be coconut milk for drinking, sold in a carton. However, coconut milk from a can is fine; just make sure you shake it thoroughly before using – it is often fairly thick so you may need to use a bit less than the recipe states. It is also possible to use coconut milk powder (follow the instructions on the packet to reconstitute it with water), diluted coconut cream, or even a solid block of creamed coconut that you can grate and dissolve into warm milk. You may need to adjust the quantities slightly to get the level of coconut flavour you enjoy.

The best substitute for coconut cream is the thickest part of a can of coconut milk. Open the can without shaking it – the thickest part of the liquid is usually at the top and you should be able to scoop it out with a spoon.

This is a non-alcoholic deep pink-red cordial originally made from pomegranates, although it does not have a strong fruit flavour. You can make your own by placing 500 ml (17 fl oz) pomegranate juice in a saucepan with 200 g (7 oz) white sugar and 2 teaspoons lemon juice, heat it gently to dissolve the sugar, then simmer until slightly syrupy in texture. Leave to cool and store in a sterilized bottle in the fridge.

If you don't want (or have time) to make grenadine, other red berry cordials can be substituted, with resulting differences in flavour, or use pomegranate juice sweetened with runny honey (make sure you stir the pomegranate juice and honey together well before adding them to the drink).

Gin

 **Fresh mint**

Some traditional cocktails specifically call for Plymouth or London gin. These are both dry styles of gin and can be used interchangeably; the main difference is that Plymouth gin is brewed using more botanicals and is often described as having an earthier, slightly less dry flavour.

Old Tom is an old-fashioned, slightly sweeter and more aromatic style of gin that is gaining popularity. It can also be used in gin-based cocktails; the difference will be more noticeable, but the cocktail will still be delicious.

In some cases, it's possible to use mint jelly instead of fresh mint. This is not recommended for cocktails where mint is the dominant flavour, such as a Mojito (see page 55), but in cocktails where the mint is balanced against another strong flavour, such as pineapple or mango, it works surprisingly well. Make sure you're using mint jelly, not mint sauce; the latter's vinegary taste will not enhance your cocktail.

GLASSWARE

Most people have a set of wine glasses, some mismatched tumblers and maybe a set of Champagne flutes in the cupboard. While you can still make a cracking cocktail using glasses you already have, serving your corner-shop cocktail in its ideal glass will elevate the experience even further. Here is a guide to the most common forms of cocktail glassware.

Short tumbler

Also called a rocks, lowball or old-fashioned glass, this sturdy glass is ideal for straight spirits and muddled drinks, like the Bourbon Peach Smash (see page 85).

Tall tumbler

Also known as a highball, this glass is a Jack-of-all-trades, as it can be used for straight mixer drinks, such as vodka and tonic, as well as any long cocktail.

Martini glass

This is the classically recognizable cocktail glass and it's used for so much more than just a Martini – so it won't sit in the back of the cupboard gathering dust. With its distinctive triangular shape and delicate stem, it's sophisticated enough to play host to the most extravagant drink in your repertoire.

Margarita glass

If you know you'll be making Margaritas often (see page 107), then it's worth investing in a few Margarita glasses to show the drinks off at their best. You can also use these glasses for Daiquiris (see page 49) and other drinks with fruit garnishes.

Champagne flute

The long, elegant lines help to keep the bubbles intact in sparkling drinks, hence their natural partnership with Champagne.

Shot glass

These are used for quick-hit drinks, which can be simple single or double servings of spirits and carefully layered creations, such as the Flat Liner (see page 125).

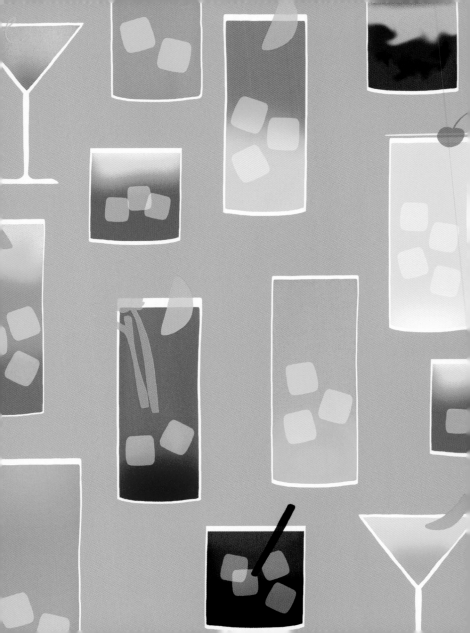

VODKA

Seabreeze

Ingredients

- handful ice cubes
- 2 measures vodka
- 4 measures cranberry juice
- 2 measures pink grapefruit juice
- 2 lime wedges

Ideal glass: tall tumbler

Method

1. Put the ice cubes in a tall tumbler.
2. Pour over the vodka and fruit juices.
3. Squeeze the lime wedges into the drink and stir with a long spoon or chopstick before serving.

Hack it!

- Instead of pink grapefruit juice, use 1 measure pomegranate juice mixed with ½ measure lemon juice and 1 teaspoon sugar syrup or honey.
- Use lemon wedges or fresh mint instead of the lime wedges.

Screwdriver

Ingredients

- 2–3 ice cubes
- 1½ measures vodka
- about 200 ml (7 fl oz) freshly squeezed orange juice, to top up

Ideal glass: tall tumbler

Method

1. Put the ice cubes in a tall tumbler.
2. Pour over the vodka, top up with orange juice and stir lightly, then serve.

Hack it!

Although freshly squeezed is better, orange juice from a carton will do the job too. However, because the ingredients are minimal, it's important to use the best-quality orange juice you can find.

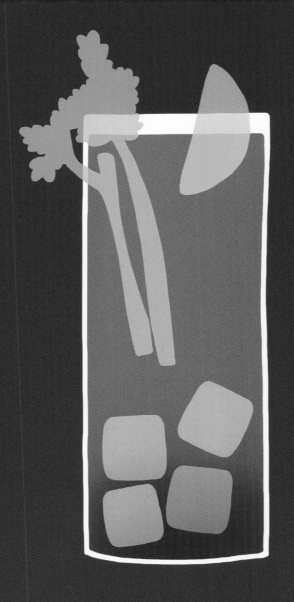

Bloody Mary

Ingredients

- handful ice cubes
- 2 measures vodka
- 1 dash lemon juice
- bottled tomato juice, to top up
- few dashes Worcestershire sauce, to taste
- ½ teaspoon ground cayenne pepper
- salt, to taste

Hack it!

- If you don't have freshly squeezed lemon juice, you can use bottled.
- Instead of Worcestershire sauce, try using Maggi liquid seasoning or any chilli sauce (but omit the cayenne pepper if using chilli sauce).
- 2 shakes Tabasco or ground black pepper can be used in place of cayenne pepper.

Method

1. Put the ice cubes in a glass.
2. Pour over the vodka and lemon juice, then top up with tomato juice and stir.
3. Add Worcestershire sauce to taste then add the cayenne pepper.
4. Season to taste with salt, then stir well to combine and chill.
5. Decorate as you wish and serve.

Ideal glass: tall tumbler

Feeling fancy?

Decorate with a celery stalk, lemon slice or cherry tomato.

Vodka Collins

Ingredients

- large handful ice cubes
- 2 measures vodka
- 2 tablespoons lime or lemon juice
- 1 teaspoon caster sugar
- soda water, to top up

Ideal glass: tall tumbler

Method

1. Half-fill a cocktail shaker or jar with a lid with ice cubes.

2. Add the vodka, lime or lemon juice and sugar and shake for at least 10 seconds; if using a metal shaker, a frost should form on the outside.

3. Strain into a tall tumbler, add the remaining ice cubes and top up with soda water.

4. Decorate as you wish, then serve.

Hack it!

Grapefruit juice can be used in place of the lime or lemon juice.

Feeling fancy?

Finish this drink off by adding a maraschino cherry and a slice of lime or lemon.

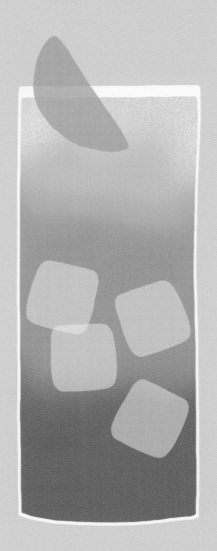

Sex on the Beach

Ingredients

- large handful ice cubes
- 1 measure vodka
- 1 measure peach schnapps
- 1 measure cranberry juice
- 1 measure orange juice

Ideal glass: tall tumbler

Method

1. Put a handful of ice cubes in a cocktail shaker or jar with a lid and add the vodka, peach schnapps, cranberry juice and orange juice.

2. Shake well for at least 10 seconds; if using a metal shaker, a frost should form on the outside.

3. Put 3–4 ice cubes in a tall tumbler and strain the liquid over the top.

4. Decorate as you wish and serve with a straw.

Feeling fancy?

- Add one measure pineapple juice along with the other liquids.

- A little bit of fruit makes a great garnish; decorate with orange, lemon or lime slices.

Cosmopolitan

Ingredients

- 6 ice cubes, cracked
- 1 measure vodka
- ½ measure Cointreau
- 1 measure cranberry juice
- 1 tablespoon lime juice

Ideal glass: martini glass

Method

1. Put the cracked ice in a cocktail shaker or jar with a lid.

2. Add all the remaining ingredients and shake for about 10 seconds; if using a metal shaker, a frost should form on the outside.

3. Strain into a cocktail glass.

4. Decorate as you wish and serve.

Feeling fancy?

- Make sure your cocktail glass is chilled before serving – it will make all the difference.

- A citrus peel twist is an easy decoration that will elevate your drink. To make one, pare a long strip of citrus peel with a vegetable peeler. Firmly twist the peel and hold it for a minute or two, then add it to your cocktail.

Hack it!

- If Cointreau isn't available, use any other orange liqueur (see page 10).

- Grapefruit juice, either fresh or from a carton, can be used instead of lime juice.

White Russian

Ingredients

- large handful ice cubes, cracked
- 1 measure vodka
- 1 measure Tia Maria
- 1 measure full-fat milk or single cream

Ideal glass: short tumbler

Method

1. Put half the cracked ice in a cocktail shaker or jar with a lid.

2. Add all the remaining ingredients and shake for at least 10 seconds; if using a metal shaker, a frost should form on the outside.

3. Put the remaining ice in a glass, strain the liquid over the top and serve with a straw.

Hack it!

Kahlúa can be used as a substitute for Tia Maria. Alternatively, use 1 measure coffee sweetened with a little sugar (in which case, add another ½ measure vodka).

Feeling fancy?

Dust over a little cocoa powder or ground nutmeg before serving.

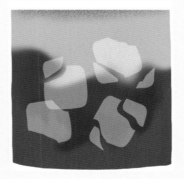

Black Russian

Ingredients

- 4–6 ice cubes, cracked
- 2 measures vodka
- 1 measure Kahlúa

Ideal glass: short tumbler

Method

1. Put the cracked ice in a short tumbler.
2. Pour over the vodka and Kahlúa, then stir.
3. Decorate as you wish and serve.

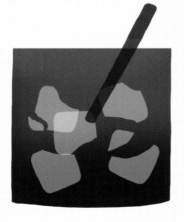

Hack it!

Tia Maria can be used as a substitute for Kahlúa.

Feeling fancy?

- Top up this cocktail with cola before serving.
- Decorate with a chocolate stick, such as a flake, for a sweet finish.

Bay Breeze

Ingredients

- large handful ice cubes
- 4 measures cranberry juice
- 2 measures vodka
- 2 measures pineapple juice

Ideal glass: tall tumbler

Method

1. Fill a glass with ice cubes and pour over the cranberry juice.

2. Put another handful of ice cubes in a cocktail shaker or jar with a lid and pour in the vodka and pineapple juice.

3. Shake well for at least 10 seconds; if using a metal shaker, a frost should form on the outside.

4. Gently strain the liquid into the glass.

5. Decorate as you wish and serve with a long straw.

Feeling fancy?

Add a lime or lemon wedge to make your drink that much prettier.

Ginger Snap

Ingredients

- 2–3 ice cubes
- 3 measures vodka
- 1 measure ginger wine
- soda water, to top up

Ideal glass: short tumbler

Method

1. Put the ice cubes in a short tumbler.
2. Pour over the vodka and ginger wine and stir gently.
3. Top up with soda water and serve.

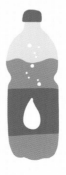

Bellini-Tini

Ingredients

- 4–5 ice cubes, cracked
- 2 measures vodka
- ½ measure peach schnapps
- 2 teaspoons peach juice
- chilled Champagne, Cava or Prosecco, to top up

Ideal glass: martini glass

Method

1. Put the cracked ice in a cocktail shaker or jar with a lid.

2. Add the vodka, schnapps and peach juice and shake well for at least 10 seconds; if using a metal shaker, a frost should form on the outside.

3. Strain into a cocktail glass and top up with chilled Champagne.

4. Decorate as you wish and serve.

Hack it!

If you can't find peach juice, use the strained juice from a can of peaches.

Feeling fancy?

- Make sure your cocktail glass is chilled before serving – it will make all the difference.

- For an added touch, decorate your drink with fresh peach slices, or use canned sliced peaches.

RUM

Tropical Treat

Ingredients

- handful ice cubes, crushed
- ½ ripe mango, peeled and stoned
- 1 measure coconut cream
- 2 measures golden or dark rum
- 1 dash fresh lemon juice
- 1 teaspoon caster sugar

Ideal glass: tall tumbler

Method

1. Put the crushed ice in a blender or food processor with all the other ingredients and blend until smooth.

2. Serve in a tall glass with a long straw and decorate as you wish.

Hack it!

- Use 100 g (3½ oz) canned or defrosted frozen mango if fresh mango is not available.

- If you don't have coconut cream, use 1½ measures coconut milk instead (see page 12).

- You can use bottled lemon juice instead of fresh.

Feeling fancy?

- Add 50 g (2 oz) fresh or frozen coconut at step 1 for an extra burst of flavour.

- Decorate your drink with some extra mango, fresh or canned.

Mai Tai

Ingredients

- large handful ice cubes, half crushed
- 2 measures golden rum
- ½ measure orange Curaçao
- ½ measure runny honey
- 2 tablespoons lime juice
- 2 teaspoons dark rum

Ideal glass: short tumbler

Hack it!

- Instead of golden rum, use 2 measures white rum mixed with ½ teaspoon light brown sugar.
- If Curaçao isn't available, use any other orange liqueur (see page 10).
- Instead of dark rum, use any rum mixed with ¼ teaspoon dark brown sugar.

Method

1. Half-fill a cocktail shaker or jar with a lid with the uncrushed ice cubes.

2. Add the golden rum, orange Curaçao, honey and lime juice to the shaker and shake for about 10 seconds; if using a metal shaker, a frost should form on the outside.

3. Put the crushed ice into a a glass and strain in the cocktail.

4. Float the dark rum on top by pouring it slowly over the back of a spoon onto the surface of the liquid.

5. Decorate as you wish and serve.

Feeling fancy?

- Add a dash of almond extract at step 2 for extra flavour.
- A lime or lemon peel twist works well as a decoration.

Spiced Mule

Ingredients

- large handful ice cubes
- 1½ measures spiced dark rum
- ½ measure lime juice
- ½ measure sugar syrup
  (see page 11 for homemade)
- ginger beer, to top up

Ideal glass: tall tumbler

Method

1. Half-fill a cocktail shaker or jar with a lid with ice cubes.

2. Add the rum, lime juice and sugar syrup to the shaker and shake well for at least 10 seconds; if using a metal shaker, a frost should form on the outside.

3. Put a handful of ice cubes in a glass and strain in the cocktail. Top with ginger beer, stirring gently.

4. Decorate as you wish and serve.

Hack it!

- If you don't have spiced dark rum, simply use any dark rum with ½ teaspoon ground allspice mixed in.

- Use grapefruit juice, either fresh or from a carton, in place of lime juice.

Feeling fancy?

Use lime or lemon wedges as a decoration.

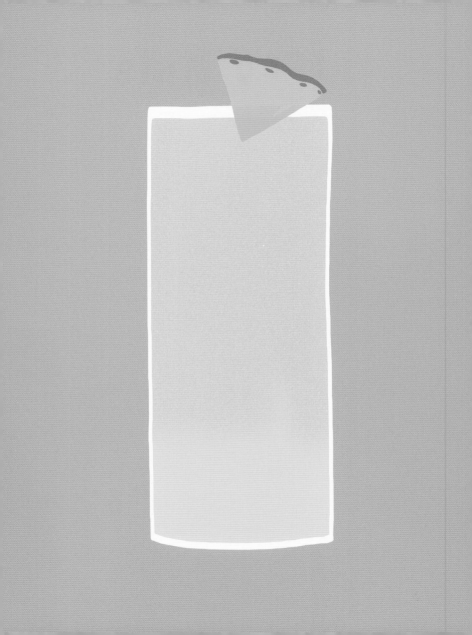

Piña Colada

Ingredients

- handful ice cubes, crushed
- 2 measures white rum
- 2 teaspoons lime juice
- 2 measures coconut cream
- 2 measures pineapple juice
- 1 scoop vanilla ice cream

Ideal glass: tall tumbler

Method

1. Put the crushed ice in a blender or food processor with all the other ingredients and blend until smooth.

2. Pour into a glass, decorate as you wish and serve.

Hack it!

- Fresh lime juice is best for this cocktail, but you can use lemon juice or bottled lime or lemon juice instead.

- If you can't find coconut cream, swap it for coconut milk (see page 12).

Feeling fancy?

Decorate with a slice of fresh or canned pineapple for a truly tropical cocktail.

Frozen Mango Daiquiri

Ingredients

- handful ice cubes, crushed
- ½ ripe mango, peeled and stoned
- 1 measure lime juice
- 1 teaspoon icing sugar
- 2 measures white rum

Ideal glass: margarita glass

Method

1. Put the crushed ice in a blender or food processor with all the other ingredients and blend until smooth.

2. Pour into a cocktail glass, decorate as you wish and serve.

Hack it!

- If you don't have fresh mango, use 100 g (3½ oz) canned or defrosted frozen mango.
- Lemon juice can be used instead of lime juice.
- Try using canned peaches instead of mango to make a peach daiquiri.

Feeling fancy?

Decorate with extra mango slices and/or some fresh mint.

Cuba Libre

Ingredients

- handful ice cubes
- 2 measures golden rum
- 1 tablespoon lime juice
- cola, to top up

Ideal glass: tall tumbler

Method

1. Fill a tall glass with ice cubes.
2. Pour the rum and lime juice into the glass and stir to chill.
3. Top up with cola, decorate as you wish and serve with a straw.

Hack it!

- Instead of golden rum, use 2 measures white rum mixed with ½ teaspoon light brown sugar.
- Instead of lime juice, you can use ¾ measure lemon or grapefruit juice.

Feeling fancy?

Decorate your drink with lime or lemon wedges.

Cuban Breeze

Ingredients

- large handful ice cubes
- 3 measures cranberry juice
- 2 measures golden rum
- 2 measures grapefruit juice

Ideal glass: tall tumbler

Method

1. Fill a tall glass with ice cubes and pour over the cranberry juice.

2. Half-fill a cocktail shaker or jar with a lid with ice cubes, add the rum and grapefruit juice and shake for at least 10 seconds; if using a metal shaker, a frost should form on the outside.

3. Strain over the cranberry juice.

4. Decorate as you wish and serve.

Hack it!

Instead of golden rum, use white rum mixed with ½ teaspoon light brown sugar.

Feeling fancy?

Lime wedges make a good decoration for this fruity drink.

St Lucia

Ingredients

- 4–5 ice cubes
- 1 measure Curaçao
- 1 measure dry vermouth
- juice of ½ orange
- 1 teaspoon grenadine
- 2 measures white or golden rum

Ideal glass: short tumbler

Hack it!

- If Curaçao isn't available, use any other orange liqueur (see page 10).
- If you don't have fresh oranges, use 2 tablespoons orange juice from a carton.
- You can use 1 tablespoon pomegranate juice mixed with ½ teaspoon honey if you don't have grenadine (see page 12).

Method

1. Put the ice cubes in a cocktail shaker or jar with a lid and add all the other ingredients.

2. Shake well for at least 10 seconds; if using a metal shaker, a frost should form on the outside.

3. Pour, without straining, into a glass.

4. Decorate as you wish and serve.

Feeling fancy?

Add a cocktail cherry or an orange peel twist for extra pizzazz.

Pineapple Mojito

Ingredients

- 6 mint leaves
- 50 g (2 oz) pineapple chunks
- 2 teaspoons soft brown sugar
- 2 measures golden rum
- handful ice cubes, crushed
- pineapple juice, to top up

Ideal glass: tall tumbler

Hack it!

- Instead of mint leaves, use 2 teaspoons mint jelly (see page 13).
- If you can't get fresh pineapple, canned works just as well.
- Instead of golden rum, use 2 measures white rum mixed with ½ teaspoon light brown sugar. Or simply use any rum you have to hand.

Method

1. Put the mint leaves in a cocktail shaker or jar with a lid along with the pineapple chunks and sugar.

2. Muddle them well to crush and combine the ingredients, then add the rum and shake well for at least 10 seconds.

3. Fill a tall glass with crushed ice, then strain the liquid over the ice. Top up with pineapple juice and stir.

4. Decorate as you wish and serve.

Feeling fancy?

A pineapple wedge and mint sprig make a lovely decoration for this drink.

Bahamas Punch

Ingredients

- 2 tablespoons lemon juice
- ½ teaspoon sugar syrup (see page 11 for homemade)
- 1–2 drops Angostura bitters
- ¼ teaspoon grenadine
- 1½ measures golden or white rum
- a few orange, lemon or pineapple slices
- handful ice cubes, cracked

Ideal glass: short tumbler

Hack it!

- Instead of using Angostura bitters, add a pinch of ground allspice or a little grated nutmeg to your cocktail.
- Use 1 tablespoon pomegranate juice mixed with ½ teaspoon honey if you don't have grenadine (see page 12).

Method

1. Put the lemon juice and sugar syrup in a cocktail shaker or jar.
2. Add the bitters, grenadine, rum and fruit. Stir well.
3. Fill a glass with cracked ice, pour in the punch without straining and serve with a straw.

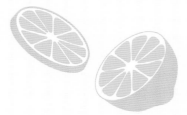

Feeling fancy?

Add a little bit of grated nutmeg to decorate your drink before serving.

Blue Hawaiian

Ingredients

- handful ice cubes, crushed
- 1 measure white rum
- ½ measure blue Curaçao
- 2 measures pineapple juice
- 1 measure coconut cream

Ideal glass: margarita glass

Method

1. Put the crushed ice in a blender or food processor with all the other ingredients and blend on a high speed until smooth.

2. Pour into a cocktail glass, decorate as you wish and serve.

Hack it!

- If blue Curaçao isn't available, use any other orange liqueur with a drop of blue food colouring (see page 10).

- If you can't get coconut cream, use 1½ measures coconut milk (see page 12).

Feeling fancy?

- Make sure your cocktail glass is chilled before serving – it will make all the difference.

- Decorate your drink with a fresh or canned pineapple wedge.

GIN

Negroni

Ingredients

- large handful ice cubes
- 1 measure dry, unflavoured gin (such as Plymouth)
- 1 measure Campari
- 1 measure red vermouth

Ideal glass: short tumbler

Method

1. Half-fill a cocktail shaker or jar with ice cubes and fill a glass with the rest.

2. Pour the gin, Campari and vermouth into the shaker or jar, stir briefly to combine and chill, then strain into the glass.

3. Decorate as you wish and serve.

Hack it!

- Aperol can be used instead of Campari.
- You can use any vermouth for this cocktail. If using white vermouth, add ½ teaspoon honey.

Feeling fancy?

- For a longer drink, top up your cocktail with soda water before serving.
- A slice of orange or lemon makes an excellent garnish.

Salty Dog

Ingredients

- 2–3 ice cubes
- pinch of salt
- 1 measure gin
- 2–2½ measures grapefruit juice

Ideal glass: short tumbler

Method

1. Put the ice cubes in a glass.

2. Add the salt, then pour over the gin and grapefruit juice and stir gently.

3. Decorate as you wish and serve.

Hack it!

You can use grapefruit juice from a carton if fresh grapefruit juice is not available.

Feeling fancy?

Decorate your drink with an orange slice or citrus peel twist.

Gin Fizz

Ingredients

- handful ice cubes
- 1 measure dry, unflavoured gin (such as Plymouth)
- 1 measure lemon juice
- 2–3 dashes sugar syrup (see page 11 for homemade)
- soda water, to top up

Ideal glass: tall tumbler

Method

1. Half-fill a cocktail shaker or jar with a lid with ice cubes.

2. Add the gin, lemon juice and sugar syrup, and shake well for about 10 seconds; if using a metal shaker, a frost should form on the outside.

3. Strain into a tall tumbler and top up with soda water.

4. Decorate as you wish and serve.

Hack it!

Fresh lemon juice is best here, but you can use bottled lemon juice if needed.

Feeling fancy?

- Try adding ¼ egg white to the cocktail shaker along with the other ingredients before shaking – it will give the drink a lovely silky mouthfeel.

- A lemon slice and mint sprig are the perfect decoration for this drink.

French 75

Ingredients

- handful ice cubes, cracked
- 1 measure gin
- 2 tablespoons lemon juice
- 1 teaspoon caster sugar
- chilled Champagne, Cava or Prosecco, to top up

Ideal glass: Champagne flute

Method

1. Half-fill a glass with cracked ice.
2. Add the gin, lemon juice and sugar and stir well.
3. Top up with chilled Champagne.
4. Decorate as you wish and serve.

Hack it!

You can use any sparkling dry white wine to top up this cocktail.

Feeling fancy?

Give this cocktail that little something extra by decorating with an orange peel twist.

Gibson

Ingredients

- 5–6 ice cubes
- ½ measure dry vermouth
- 3 measures gin
- cocktail onion, to decorate

Ideal glass: martini glass

Method

1. Put the ice cubes in a cocktail shaker or jar.

2. Pour over the vermouth and gin and stir well (never shake) to combine and chill.

3. Strain into a cocktail glass, add a cocktail onion and serve.

Feeling fancy?

- Make sure your cocktail glass is chilled before serving – it will make all the difference.

- If you don't have cocktail onions, use a small pickled onion instead.

Hack it!

This is a classic dirty twist on a gin Martini. If you fancy a Martini instead, turn to page 77.

Gimlet

Ingredients

- handful ice cubes
- 2 measures gin
- 1 measure lime cordial
- ½ measure water

Ideal glass: martini glass

Method

1. Fill a cocktail shaker or jar with ice cubes. Add the gin and lime cordial and stir well.

2. Strain into a chilled cocktail glass, add the water and serve.

Hack it!

Try experimenting with this cocktail by using other cordials in place of lime.

Feeling fancy?

- Any lime cordial will work, but if you use good-quality lime cordial you will really notice a difference in the end result.

- Use a lime wedge to decorate – squeeze it over the cocktail before adding it to the glass.

Tom Collins

Ingredients

- handful ice cubes
- 2 measures gin
- 1½ teaspoons lemon juice
- 1 teaspoon sugar syrup
  (see page 11 for homemade)
- soda water, to top up

Ideal glass: tall tumbler

Method

1. Fill a glass with ice cubes and add the gin, lemon juice and sugar syrup. Stir well.

2. Top up with soda water.

3. Decorate as you wish and serve.

Hack it!

Since this drink is so simple, it really does require freshly squeezed lemon juice.

Feeling fancy?

A lemon slice makes a simple but classy decoration.

Fair Lady

Ingredients

- handful ice cubes
- 1 measure gin
- 4 measures grapefruit juice
- 1 dash Cointreau

Ideal glass: martini glass

Method

1. Put the ice cubes in a cocktail shaker or jar with a lid and pour in the gin, grapefruit juice and Cointreau.

2. Shake well for at least 10 seconds; if using a metal shaker, a frost should form on the outside.

3. Strain into a cocktail glass and serve.

Hack it!

- Instead of Cointreau, use Grand Marnier, triple sec or any other orange liqueur (see page 10).

- Fresh grapefruit juice is best, but you can use grapefruit juice from a carton if needed.

Feeling fancy?

Frost the rim of your cocktail glass! To do this, place 1 egg white in a shallow dish and some caster sugar in another. Dip the rim of the glass into the egg white, then press it into the sugar to frost. Pour the remaining egg white into the cocktail shaker or jar along with the other cocktail ingredients before shaking – this will give the drink a lovely silky mouthfeel.

Dry Martini

Ingredients

- ½ measure dry vermouth
- 3 measures ice-cold gin

Ideal glass: martini glass

Method

1. Swirl the vermouth around the inside of a chilled cocktail glass, then discard the excess.

2. Pour in the ice-cold gin and serve.

Feeling fancy?

- Make sure your cocktail glass is chilled before serving – it will make all the difference.

- Decorate your cocktail with a brined green olive to make it a 'dirty Martini', or with a lemon peel twist for a 'Martini with a twist'.

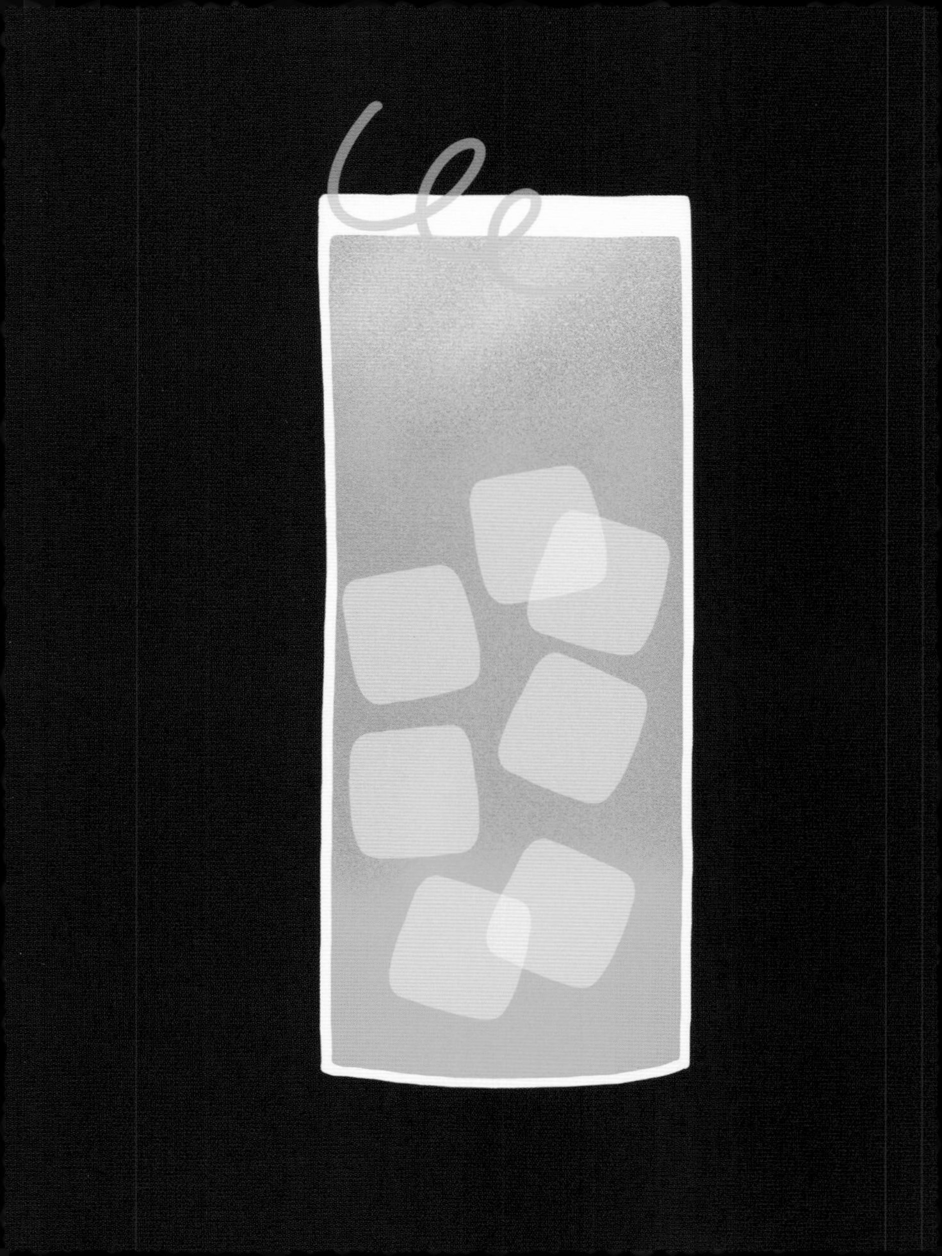

Bittersweet

Ingredients

- handful ice cubes
- 2 measures gin
- 1 tablespoon lime juice
- 2 dashes grenadine
- 1 teaspoon sugar syrup (see page 11 for homemade)
- bitter lemon, to top up

Ideal glass: tall tumbler

Method

1. Put half the ice cubes in a cocktail shaker or jar with a lid and pour over the gin, lime juice, grenadine and sugar syrup.

2. Shake well for at least 10 seconds; if using a metal shaker, a frost should form on the outside.

3. Put the remaining ice cubes in a tall glass, strain the cocktail over the ice and top up with bitter lemon.

4. Decorate as you wish and serve.

Hack it!

- Use 1 measure pomegranate juice mixed with ½ teaspoon honey or sugar syrup if you don't have grenadine (see page 12).

- Substitute bitter lemon for cloudy lemonade plus a dash of lemon juice.

Feeling fancy?

Decorate your drink with a lemon peel twist.

Gin Tropical

Ingredients

- handful ice cubes
- 1½ measures gin
- 1 measure lemon juice
- 1 measure passion fruit juice
- ½ measure orange juice
- soda water, to top up

Ideal glass: short tumbler

Method

1. Put half the ice cubes in a cocktail shaker or jar with a lid.

2. Pour the gin, lemon juice, passion fruit juice and orange juice into the shaker or jar and shake well for at least 10 seconds; if using a metal shaker, a frost should form on the outside.

3. Put the remaining ice cubes in a glass. Strain in the cocktail. Top up with soda water and stir gently.

4. Decorate as you wish and serve.

Hack it!

- Fresh lemon and orange juice are best for this, but use juice from a bottle or carton if needed.

- If passion fruit juice is scarce, use any tropical fruit juice blend.

Feeling fancy?

An orange peel twist makes the perfect garnish.

WHISKY

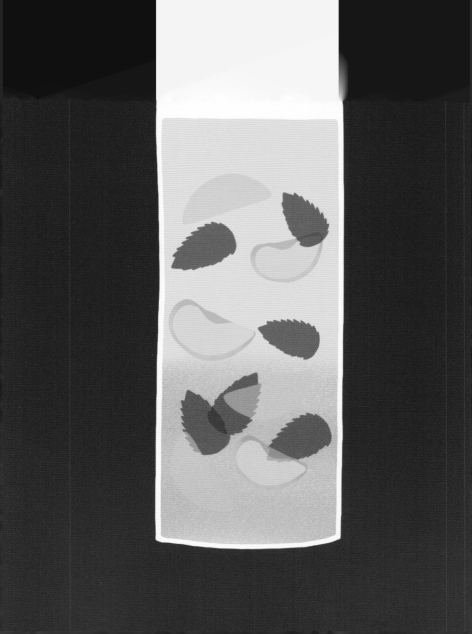

Bourbon Peach Smash

Ingredients

- 6 mint leaves
- 3 peach slices
- 3 lemon slices
- 2 teaspoons caster sugar
- large handful ice cubes, half crushed
- 2 measures Jack Daniels

Ideal glass: tall tumbler

Method

1. Put the mint leaves, peach and lemon slices and sugar in a cocktail shaker or jar with a lid and muddle together.

2. Half-fill the shaker with ice cubes and put the crushed ice in a short tumbler.

3. Add the Jack Daniels to the shaker and shake well for at least 10 seconds; if using a metal shaker, a frost should form on the outside.

4. Strain over the ice in the tumbler.

5. Decorate as you wish and serve.

Hack it!

- Instead of mint leaves, use 1 teaspoon mint jelly (see page 13).

- Instead of fresh peach, use 5 peach slices from a can.

- You can use any bourbon whiskey in place of Jack Daniels.

Feeling fancy?

Decorate with a lemon wedge before serving.

Whisky Sour

Ingredients

- handful ice cubes
- 2 measures whisky
- 1½ measures lemon juice
- 2 tablespoons caster sugar

Ideal glass: short tumbler

Hack it!

Fresh lemon juice is best for this, but you can use bottled lemon juice if needed.

Method

1. Half-fill a cocktail shaker or jar with a lid with ice cubes.

2. Add the whisky, lemon juice and sugar and shake well for at least 10 seconds; if using a metal shaker, a frost should form on the outside.

3. Fill a glass with ice cubes and strain the liquid over the top.

4. Decorate as you wish and serve.

Feeling fancy?

- Add 1 egg white and/or 4 dashes of Angostura bitters or use a pinch of ground allspice along with the other ingredients in the cocktail shaker before shaking. This will create a slightly longer drink with a lovely silky mouthfeel.

- Decorate this cocktail with a lemon or orange slice or a cocktail cherry for some extra flair.

Irish Coffee

Ingredients

- 1 measure Irish whiskey
- hot filter coffee, to top up
- double cream, lightly whipped

Ideal glass: heatproof glass

Method

1. Put a long spoon in a large heatproof glass and add the whiskey, then top up with coffee almost to the top of the glass. Stir well.

2. Rest the upturned bowl of the spoon on top of the coffee and slowly pour the cream over it. Gently pull out the spoon so that the cream floats.

3. Decorate as you wish and serve.

Hack it!

- Irish whiskey is obviously best, but you can use any whisky for this cocktail.

- Instant whipped cream works just as well in a pinch – just squirt it on the top.

Feeling fancy?

Decorate with a sprinkling of ground coffee before serving.

Mississippi Punch

Ingredients

- large handful ice cubes, crushed
- 1 teaspoon sugar syrup
  (see page 11 for homemade)
- 4 tablespoons lemon juice
- 1 measure brandy
- 1 measure dark rum
- 2 measures Jack Daniels

Ideal glass: tall tumbler

Method

1. Half-fill a tall glass with crushed ice.

2. Pour in the sugar syrup and the lemon juice, then stir gently to mix thoroughly.

3. Add the brandy, rum and Jack Daniels, in that order, stir once and serve with a straw.

Hack it!

You can use any bourbon whiskey in place of Jack Daniels.

Feeling fancy?

- Add 3 drops Angostura bitters or use a pinch of ground allspice along with the sugar syrup and lemon juice.

- Decorate with a lemon slice.

Rusty Nail

Ingredients

- handful ice cubes
- 1½–2 measures whisky
- 1 measure Drambuie

Ideal glass: short tumbler

Method

1. Fill a short tumbler with ice cubes and pour over the whisky and Drambuie.
2. Stir gently and serve.

Hack it!

If you don't have Drambuie, use 1 teaspoon honey and 1 measure orange juice (fresh or from a carton).

Godfather

Ingredients

- handful ice cubes
- 2 measures whisky
- 1 measure Disaronno

Ideal glass: short tumbler

Method

1. Fill a cocktail shaker or jar with a lid with half the ice cubes.

2. Pour the whisky and Disaronno into the shaker and shake well for at least 10 seconds; if using a metal shaker, a frost should form on the outside.

3. Put the remaining ice cubes in a glass and strain in the cocktail.

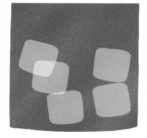

Hack it!

You can use any Amaretto in place of Disaronno.

New Yorker

Ingredients

- 2–3 ice cubes, cracked
- 1 measure whisky
- 1 teaspoon fresh lime juice
- 1 teaspoon icing sugar

Ideal glass: martini glass

Method

1. Put the cracked ice in a cocktail shaker or jar with a lid.

2. Add the whisky, lime juice and sugar and shake well for at least 10 seconds; if using a metal shaker, a frost should form on the outside.

3. Strain into a cocktail glass, decorate as you wish and serve.

Hack it!

Fresh lime juice is best for this, but use bottled lime juice if needed. Alternatively, use lemon juice.

Feeling fancy?

Finely grate a little lemon zest over the top of this cocktail before serving and/or add a lemon peel twist to the rim of the glass.

Capricorn

Ingredients

- 4–5 ice cubes, cracked
- 1 measure Jack Daniels
- ½ measure apricot brandy
- ½ measure lemon juice
- 2 measures orange juice

Ideal glass: short tumbler

Method

1. Put half the cracked ice cubes in a cocktail shaker or jar with a lid and add the Jack Daniels, apricot brandy and the lemon and orange juices. Shake to mix.

2. Put the remaining ice in a short tumbler and strain over the cocktail.

3. Decorate as you wish and serve.

Hack it!

- You can use any bourbon whiskey in place of Jack Daniels.
- If you don't have apricot brandy, use 1 measure peach schnapps instead.
- Fresh lemon and orange juice are best for this, but you can use juice from a bottle or carton if needed.

Feeling fancy?

Decorate your cocktail with an orange slice.

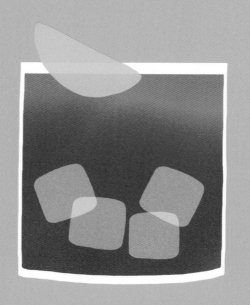

Rhett Butler

Ingredients

- large handful ice cubes
- 2 measures Jack Daniels
- 4 measures cranberry juice
- 2 tablespoons sugar syrup (see page 11 for homemade)
- 1 tablespoon fresh lime juice

Ideal glass: short tumbler

Method

1. Put 4–5 ice cubes in a cocktail shaker or jar with a lid and add the Jack Daniels, cranberry juice, sugar syrup and lime juice.

2. Shake well for at least 10 seconds; if using a metal shaker, a frost should form on the outside.

3. Fill a short tumbler with the remaining ice cubes and strain over the cocktail.

4. Decorate as you wish and serve with a straw.

Hack it!

- You can use any bourbon whiskey in place of Jack Daniels.
- Instead of fresh lime juice, use fresh lemon juice.

Feeling fancy?

Decorate your glass with a lime slice or wedge.

Southerly Buster

Ingredients

- 4–5 ice cubes
- 1 measure blue Curaçao
- 3 measures whisky

Ideal glass: martini glass

Method

1. Put the ice cubes in a cocktail shaker or jar.
2. Add the Curaçao and whisky, stir vigorously, then strain into a cocktail glass.
3. Decorate as you wish and serve.

Hack it!

If blue Curaçao is not available, use any other orange liqueur with a dash of blue food colouring (see page 10).

Feeling fancy?

- Make sure your cocktail glass is chilled before serving – it will make all the difference.
- Decorate your cocktail with a lemon peel twist.

Vanilla Daisy

Ingredients

- handful ice cubes, crushed
- 2 measures Jack Daniels
- 1 measure fresh lemon juice
- 1 measure vanilla syrup
- 1 teaspoon grenadine

Ideal glass: short tumbler

Hack it!

- You can use any bourbon whiskey in place of Jack Daniels.

- If you don't have vanilla syrup, try using 1 measure sugar syrup (see page 11 for homemade) or honey mixed with 1 teaspoon vanilla extract.

- You can use 1 tablespoon pomegranate juice mixed with ½ teaspoon honey if you don't have grenadine (see page 12).

Method

1. Put half the crushed ice in a cocktail shaker or jar with a lid.

2. Add the Jack Daniels, lemon juice and vanilla syrup to the shaker and shake well for at least 10 seconds; if using a metal shaker, a frost should form on the outside.

3. Put the remaining crushed ice in a glass and strain in the cocktail. Drizzle the grenadine over the top.

4. Decorate as you wish and serve.

Feeling fancy?

Top your drink with 2 maraschino cherries before serving.

TEQUILA

Berry Margarita

Ingredients

- handful ice cubes, crushed
- 1 measure tequila
- 1 measure triple sec
- 1 measure strawberry liqueur
- 1 measure fresh lime juice
- 12 strawberries, hulled

Ideal glass: margarita glass

Method

1. Put the crushed ice in a blender or food processor with all the other ingredients and blend on a high speed until smooth but slushy.

2. Pour into a cocktail glass.

3. Decorate as you wish and serve.

Feeling fancy?

- Make sure your cocktail glass is chilled before serving – it will make all the difference.

- Decorate your cocktail with fresh or frozen strawberries or raspberries.

Hack it!

- If triple sec isn't available, use any other orange liqueur (see page 10).

- If strawberry liqueur is scarce, use ½ measure vodka mixed with 2 teaspoons strawberry or raspberry jam.

- Fresh lemon juice can be used instead of fresh lime juice.

- If you can't get fresh strawberries, use frozen strawberries and/or raspberries.

Dirty Sanchez

Ingredients

- handful ice cubes
- 2 teaspoons dry vermouth
- 2 measures tequila
- 2 teaspoons brine from a jar of black olives

Ideal glass: martini glass

Method

1. Fill a cocktail shaker or jar with ice cubes and add the vermouth.

2. Stir to coat the ice, then strain and discard the excess vermouth.

3. Pour the tequila and brine over the ice and stir until thoroughly chilled.

4. Strain into a cocktail glass and decorate as you wish.

Hack it!

Aged or gold tequila is best for this, but any tequila will do.

Feeling fancy?

- Make sure your cocktail glass is chilled before serving – it will make all the difference.

- Add 2 black olives, to decorate.

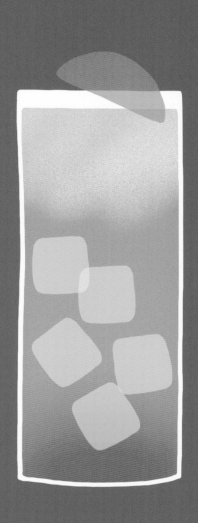

Tequila Sunrise

Ingredients

- handful ice cubes
- 2 measures tequila
- 4 measures orange juice
- 2 teaspoons grenadine

Ideal glass: tall tumbler

Method

1. Put the ice cubes in a cocktail shaker or a jar with a lid, add the tequila and orange juice and shake well for at least 10 seconds; if using a metal shaker, a frost should form on the outside.

2. Fill a tall tumbler with ice cubes and strain the liquid over the top. Slowly pour in the grenadine and allow it to settle.

3. Decorate as you wish and serve.

Hack it!

- Fresh orange juice is best for this, but you can use juice from a carton if needed.
- You can use 2 teaspoons pomegranate juice mixed with 1 teaspoon honey or sugar syrup if you don't have grenadine (see page 12).

Feeling fancy?

Decorate your drink with orange or lemon slices for a fancy finish.

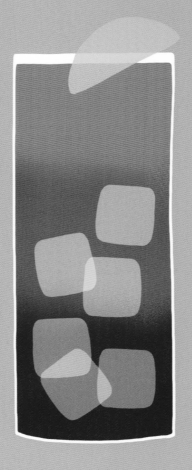

El Diablo

Ingredients

- handful ice cubes
- 1¼ measures tequila
- ¾ measure fresh lime juice
- 2 teaspoons grenadine
- ginger ale, to top up

Ideal glass: tall tumbler

Hack it!

- Aged or gold tequila is best for this, but any tequila will do.
- Instead of fresh lime juice, use fresh lemon juice.
- You can use 1 tablespoon pomegranate juice mixed with ½ teaspoon honey if you don't have grenadine (see page 12).
- Feel free to switch the ginger ale for ginger beer.

Method

1. Fill a tall tumbler with ice cubes.
2. Pour over the tequila, lime juice and grenadine.
3. Top up with ginger ale and stir gently.
4. Decorate as you wish and serve.

Feeling fancy?

Add a lime slice or wedge to the rim of the glass.

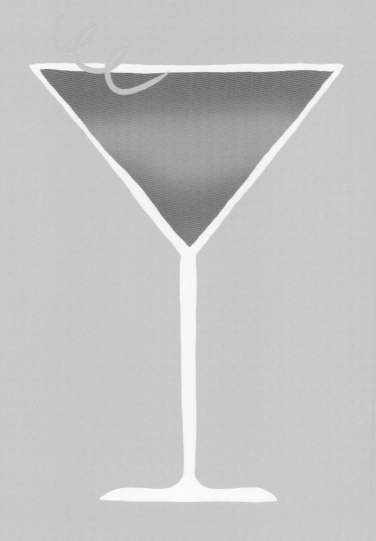

Rude Cosmopolitan

Ingredients

- handful ice cubes
- 1½ measures tequila
- 1 measure Cointreau
- 1 measure cranberry juice
- ½ measure fresh lime juice

Ideal glass: martini glass

Method

1. Put the ice cubes in a cocktail shaker or jar with a lid.
2. Add all the remaining ingredients and shake well for at least 10 seconds; if using a metal shaker, a frost should form on the outside.
3. Strain into a cocktail glass.
4. Decorate as you wish and serve.

Hack it!

- Aged or gold tequila is best for this, but any tequila will do.
- If Cointreau isn't available, use any other orange liqueur (see page 10).
- Fresh lemon juice can be used in place of lime juice.

Feeling fancy?

You can flame an orange twist to decorate this drink, to add a bit of theatre and help release the scent. Pare a large strip of orange peel with a wide vegetable peeler, hold it over the glass with one hand and hold a long, lighted match in the other hand. Twist the peel firmly so that the oils spray into the flame and ignite, then drop it into the drink.

Pancho Villa

Ingredients

- 4–5 ice cubes
- 1 measure tequila
- ½ measure Tia Maria
- 1 teaspoon Cointreau

Ideal glass: martini glass

Method

1. Put the ice cubes in a cocktail shaker or jar with a lid and pour in the tequila, Tia Maria and Cointreau.

2. Shake well for at least 10 seconds; if using a metal shaker, a frost should form on the outside.

3. Strain into a cocktail glass and serve.

Hack it!

- Instead of Tia Maria, you can use Kahlúa.

- If Cointreau isn't available, use any other orange liqueur (see page 10).

Feeling fancy?

Make sure your cocktail glass is chilled before serving – it will make all the difference.

Brave Bull

Ingredients

- handful ice cubes
- ¾ measure tequila
- ¾ measure Kahlúa

Ideal glass: short tumbler

Method

1. Fill a glass with ice cubes.
2. Pour in the tequila and Kahlúa and stir gently before serving.

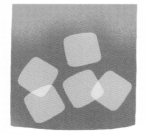

Hack it!

Instead of Kahlúa, you can use Tia Maria.

Pink Cadillac Convertible

Ingredients

- fine sea salt
- 3 lime wedges
- handful ice cubes
- 1¼ measures tequila
- ½ measure cranberry juice
- ¾ measure Grand Marnier

Ideal glass: short tumbler

Hack it!

- Aged or gold tequila is best for this, but any tequila will do.
- You can use lemon wedges instead of lime if needed.
- If Grand Marnier isn't available, use any other orange liqueur (see page 10).

Method

1. Place a little salt in a shallow dish. Frost the rim of a short tumbler by moistening it with a lime or lemon wedge, then pressing it into the salt. Fill the glass with ice cubes.

2. Pour the tequila and cranberry juice into a cocktail shaker or jar with a lid.

3. Squeeze over the juice from the remaining lime wedges, pressing the rind to release its oils, then drop the wedges into the shaker. Add 4–5 ice cubes and shake vigorously for at least 10 seconds; if using a metal shaker, a frost should form on the outside.

4. Strain the liquid into the glass, then drizzle the Grand Marnier over the top and decorate as you wish.

Feeling fancy?

Use an extra lime wedge to decorate your cocktail.

Mexicana

Ingredients

- 8–10 ice cubes
- 1¼ measures tequila
- ¾ measure framboise liqueur
- ¾ measure fresh lemon juice
- 3½ measures pineapple juice

Ideal glass: tall tumbler

Method

1. Put half the ice cubes with the tequila, framboise liqueur and fruit juices in a cocktail shaker or jar with a lid and shake well for at least 10 seconds; if using a metal shaker, a frost should form on the outside.

2. Put the remaining ice cubes in a tall glass, strain the cocktail over the top and decorate as you wish.

Hack it!

This cocktail uses framboise liqueur, which is a sweet, red, raspberry-flavoured liqueur made in France. If you can't find it, muddle 5 fresh, canned or frozen raspberries with ¼ teaspoon honey and ½ measure vodka, then strain the mixture into the cocktail shaker or jar to remove any seeds.

Feeling fancy?

Add a pineapple wedge and lemon slice for decoration.

Ruby Rita

Ingredients

- fine sea salt
- 1¼ measures pink grapefruit juice
- handful ice cubes
- 1¼ measures tequila
- ¾ measure Cointreau

Ideal glass: short tumbler

Hack it!

- Aged or gold tequila is best for this, but any tequila will do.
- Fresh grapefruit juice is best for this, but you can use juice from a carton if needed.
- If Cointreau isn't available, use any other orange liqueur (see page 10).

Method

1. Place a little salt in a shallow dish. Frost the rim of a short tumbler by moistening it with some of the pink grapefruit juice and pressing it into the salt. Fill the glass with ice cubes.

2. Pour the tequila, Cointreau and the remaining pink grapefruit juice into a cocktail shaker or jar with a lid, fill with ice and shake well for at least 10 seconds; if using a metal shaker, a frost should form on the outside.

3. Strain into the prepared glass and decorate as you wish.

Feeling fancy?

Add a pink grapefruit wedge, to decorate.

Flat Liner

Ingredients

- ¾ measure gold tequila
- 4 drops Tabasco sauce
- ¾ measure sambuca

Ideal glass: shot glass

Method

1. Pour the tequila into a shot glass.

2. Hold a metal spoon close to the surface of the liquid, convex side up.

3. Slowly add the Tabasco over the back of the spoon so that it floats on top of the tequila.

4. Add the sambuca in the same way so that it forms a layer on top.

5. Drink it in one.

Hack it!

- Any hot sauce can be used in this cocktail so switch out Tabasco for whatever you have to hand.

- You can use any aniseed liqueur in place of sambuca.

BRANDY

Brandy Sidecar

Ingredients

- handful ice cubes
- 1 measure Cointreau
- 2 measures brandy
- 1 measure fresh lemon juice

Ideal glass: martini glass

Method

1. Half-fill a cocktail shaker or jar with a lid with ice cubes.

2. Add the remaining ingredients and shake for at least 10 seconds; if using a metal shaker, a frost should form on the outside.

3. Strain into a cocktail glass.

4. Decorate as you wish and serve.

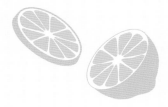

Hack it!

If Cointreau isn't available, use any other orange liqueur (see page 10).

Feeling fancy?

- Make sure your cocktail glass is chilled before serving – it will make all the difference.

- To decorate, add a maraschino cherry and an orange or lemon peel twist.

Scorpion

Ingredients

- handful ice cubes, crushed
- 1 measure brandy
- ½ measure white rum
- ½ measure dark rum
- 2 measures fresh orange juice
- 2 teaspoons Amaretto

Ideal glass: tall tumbler

Method

1. Put half the crushed ice in a cocktail shaker or jar with a lid and add the brandy, rums, orange juice and Amaretto.

2. Shake well for at least 10 seconds; if using a metal shaker, a frost should form on the outside.

3. Place the remaining ice in a tall glass and strain over the liquid.

4. Decorate as you wish and serve with a straw.

Hack it!

Fresh orange juice is best for this recipe, but you can use juice from a carton if needed.

Feeling fancy?

- Add 2–3 dashes Angostura bitters or a pinch of ground allspice with all the other ingredients in the cocktail shaker.

- Decorate the glass with orange or lemon slices.

Brandy Alexander

Ingredients

- handful ice cubes, cracked
- 1 measure brandy
- 1 measure dark crème de cacao
- 1 measure single cream

Ideal glass: martini glass

Method

1. Put the cracked ice in a cocktail shaker or jar with a lid.

2. Add all the remaining ingredients and shake well for at least 10 seconds; if using a metal shaker, a frost should form on the outside.

3. Strain into a cocktail glass. Decorate as you wish and serve.

Hack it!

- Instead of crème de cacao, use 1 measure shop-bought chocolate sauce mixed with 1 teaspoon vodka.

- Long-life cream works fine in this recipe. Alternatively, you can use coconut cream (see page 12).

- Try making a Frozen Alexander: place all the ingredients in a blender or food processor, substituting the cream for about 2 tablespoons vanilla ice cream, and blend until smooth.

Feeling fancy?

- Make sure your cocktail glass is chilled before serving – it will make all the difference.

- Decorate with a chocolate flake and/or a dusting of cocoa powder to complete this sweet after-dinner drink.

Bedtime Bouncer

Ingredients

- 2 measures brandy
- 1 measure Cointreau
- 5 measures bitter lemon
- 4–6 ice cubes

Ideal glass: short tumbler

Method

1. Pour the brandy, Cointreau and bitter lemon into a short tumbler, stir well and add the ice.

2. Decorate as you wish and serve with a straw.

Hack it!

- If Cointreau isn't available, use any other orange liqueur (see page 10).

- Rather than bitter lemon, use 2 measures cloudy lemonade and 1 measure lemon juice.

Feeling fancy?

A lemon peel twist makes a great garnish for this cocktail.

Brandy Sour

Ingredients

- handful ice cubes
- 2 tablespoons lemon juice
- 3 measures brandy
- 1 teaspoon sugar syrup
  (see page 11 for homemade)

Ideal glass: short tumbler

Method

1. Put half the ice cubes in a cocktail shaker or jar with a lid.

2. Add all the remaining ingredients and shake well for at least 10 seconds; if using a metal shaker, a frost should form on the outside.

3. Put the rest of the ice cubes in a short tumbler, strain over the cocktail and decorate as you wish. Serve with a straw.

Feeling fancy?

- Add 3 drops Angostura bitters or use a pinch of ground allspice along with the other ingredients.
- Thread lemon slices onto a cocktail stick, to decorate.

Brandy Fix

Ingredients

- handful ice cubes, crushed
- 2 teaspoons sugar syrup
  (see page 11 for homemade)
- 1¼ measures fresh lemon juice
- ½ measure cherry brandy
- 1 measure brandy

Ideal glass: short tumbler

Method

1. Fill a short tumbler with crushed ice.
2. Add all the ingredients, one by one in the order specified, over the ice.
3. Decorate as you wish and serve.

Hack it!

Rather than cherry brandy, use ½ measure brandy muddled with 1 teaspoon cherry jam.

Feeling fancy?

Add a lemon peel twist, to decorate.

Tidal Wave

Ingredients

- 6 ice cubes
- 1 measure Mandarine Napoléon
- 4 measures bitter lemon
- 1 dash fresh lemon juice

Ideal glass: short tumbler

Method

1. Put the ice cubes in a short tumbler.
2. Add the Mandarine Napoléon, bitter lemon and lemon juice and stir well.
3. Decorate as you wish and serve.

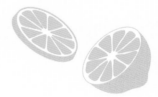

Hack it!

- If Mandarine Napoléon is too hard to find, you can use Grand Marnier, or brandy mixed with 1 teaspoon orange juice.
- Instead of bitter lemon, use 3 measures cloudy lemonade mixed with 1 teaspoon lemon juice.

Feeling fancy?

Decorate with a lemon slice.

Brandy Flip

Ingredients

- handful ice cubes
- 1 egg
- 2 measures brandy
- 1½ teaspoons caster sugar

Ideal glass: martini glass

Method

1. Half-fill a cocktail shaker or jar with a lid with ice cubes.
2. Add all the remaining ingredients and shake well for at least 10 seconds; if using a metal shaker, a frost should form on the outside.
3. Strain into a cocktail glass.
4. Decorate as you wish and serve.

Feeling fancy?

Decorate your drink with freshly grated nutmeg, or ground cinnamon or allspice.

Apple Posset

Ingredients

- 8 measures unsweetened apple juice
- 1 teaspoon soft brown sugar
- 2 tablespoons Calvados
- cinnamon stick

Ideal glass: heatproof glass

Method

1. Heat the apple juice in a small saucepan to just below boiling point.

2. Meanwhile, measure the sugar and Calvados into a warmed heatproof glass.

3. Add the hot apple juice.

4. Stir with the cinnamon stick until the sugar has dissolved, then serve.

Hack it!

- Calvados is best for this, but you can use any brandy.

- If you do not have a cinnamon stick, add a pinch of ground cinnamon along with the hot apple juice and stir everything with a spoon instead.

Leo

Ingredients

- handful ice cubes
- 1 measure brandy
- 1½ measures fresh orange juice
- ½ measure Amaretto
- soda water, to taste
- 1 teaspoon Campari

Ideal glass: tall tumbler

Method

1. Put the ice in a cocktail shaker or jar with a lid.

2. Add the brandy, orange juice and Amaretto and shake well for at least 10 seconds; if using a metal shaker, a frost should form on the outside.

3. Strain into a tall glass with ice, add soda water to taste, then drizzle over the Campari.

Hack it!

- Fresh orange juice is best for this recipe, but you can use juice from a carton if needed.

- If you don't have Campari, use Aperol instead.

Bouncing Bomb

Ingredients

- 4–5 ice cubes
- 2 measures brandy
- 1 measure Curaçao
- soda water, to top up

Ideal glass: short tumbler

Method

1. Put the ice cubes in a cocktail shaker or mixing glass.

2. Pour the brandy and Curaçao over the ice and stir vigorously.

3. Strain into a short tumbler and top up with soda water.

4. Decorate as you wish and serve.

Hack it!

If Curaçao isn't available, use any other orange liqueur (see page 10).

Feeling fancy?

Add an orange peel twist to decorate your drink.

WINE & OTHER SPIRITS

Pimm's Cocktail

Ingredients

- handful ice cubes
- 1 measure Pimm's No 1
- 1 measure gin
- 2 measures lemonade
- 2 measures ginger ale
- any combination of cucumber slices, blueberries, strawberries, fresh mint, lemon or orange slices

Ideal glass: tall tumbler

Method

1. Fill a tall tumbler with ice cubes.
2. Add all the remaining liquids, in the order specified, over the ice.
3. Stir in the fruit and serve.

Hack it!

- If ginger ale is too tricky to locate, use ginger beer.
- If you don't have the fruit mentioned above, add whatever you have, such as grapes, pear, nectarine, or even frozen berries.

Long Island Iced Tea

Ingredients

- handful ice cubes
- ½ measure vodka
- ½ measure gin
- ½ measure white rum
- ½ measure tequila
- ½ measure Cointreau
- ½ measure lemon juice
- cola, to top up

Ideal glass: tall tumbler

Method

1. Half-fill a cocktail shaker or jar with a lid with ice cubes.

2. Pour the vodka, gin, rum, tequila, Cointreau and lemon juice into the shaker and shake well for at least 10 seconds; if using a metal shaker, a frost should form on the outside.

3. Fill a tall glass with ice cubes and strain over the cocktail. Top up with cola.

4. Decorate as you wish and serve.

Hack it!

If Cointreau isn't available, use any other orange liqueur (see page 10).

Feeling fancy?

Add a lemon wedge to the rim of your glass before serving.

Sangria

Ingredients

- large handful ice cubes
- 2 bottles (1.5 litres/2¾ pints) light Spanish red wine, chilled
- 450 ml (¾ pint) soda water, chilled
- 200 g (7 oz) seasonal fruit, such as apples, pears, lemons, peaches and strawberries, sliced

Serves 10–12

Ideal glass: tall tumbler

Method

1. Put the ice cubes in a large bowl and pour over the wine. Stir well.

2. Add the soda water and float the fruit on top.

3. Use a ladle to serve the sangria in tall glasses.

Hack it!

Instead of Spanish red wine, use any light red wine such as Pinot Noir, Grenache, Zinfandel or Beaujolais.

Feeling fancy?

- Decorate your glass with orange or lemon slices for a fruity finish.
- Add 4 measures brandy or dark rum along with the wine.

White Sangria

Ingredients

- 2 large glasses dry white wine
- 2 measures lemon vodka
- 2 measures peach schnapps
- 2 measures peach purée
- 200 g (7 oz) apple, lime, lemon and peach slices
- handful ice cubes
- 1 measure fresh lemon juice
- 1 measure fresh lime juice
- lemonade, to top up

Serves 6
Ideal glass: short tumbler

Method

1. 12 hours before serving, put the wine, vodka, schnapps, peach purée and fruit slices in a jug and stir to mix. Cover and chill in the refrigerator.

2. Just before serving, add some ice cubes and the fruit juices and top up with lemonade.

3. Serve from the jug into short tumblers.

Hack it!

- Instead of lemon vodka, use ordinary vodka.
- Puréed canned peaches do the job just as well as peach purée.
- You can use any pale-coloured fruit, such as pear, white grapes or white nectarine.
- If you cannot find fresh limes, use extra lemon juice, or bottled lime juice.

Grand Mimosa

Ingredients

- 2–3 ice cubes
- 1 measure Grand Marnier
- 2 measures fresh orange juice
- chilled Champagne, Cava or Prosecco, to top up

Ideal glass: Champagne flute

Method

1. Put the ice cubes in a cocktail shaker or jar, pour in the Grand Marnier and orange juice and stir well to chill.

2. Strain into a Champagne flute and top up with the Champagne, Cava or Prosecco.

Hack it!

- If Grand Marnier isn't available, use any other orange liqueur with a dash of brandy added (see page 10).

- Fresh orange juice is best for this recipe, but you can use juice from a carton if needed.

Index

Glossary

UK	US
Sieve	Strainer
Tea towel	Dish towel
Jam	Jelly
Jam jar	Jelly jar
Soda water	Seltzer water
Caster sugar	Superfine sugar

UK	US
Icing sugar	Confectioner's or powdered sugar
Double cream	Heavy cream
Single cream	Light cream
Whisky	Scotch whisky
Whiskey	Irish or American whiskey

hamlyn

First published in Great Britain in 2024 by Hamlyn, an imprint of Octopus Publishing Group Ltd
Carmelite House, 50 Victoria Embankment
London EC4Y 0DZ
www.octopusbooks.co.uk

An Hachette UK Company
www.hachette.co.uk

This book contains material previously published in *The Classic Cocktail Bible* and *HAC: 200 Classic Cocktails*

Copyright © Octopus Publishing Group Ltd 2024

Distributed in the US by Hachette Book Group
1290 Avenue of the Americas, 4th and 5th Floors
New York, NY 10104

Distributed in Canada by Canadian Manda Group
664 Annette St., Toronto, Ontario, Canada M6S 2C8

ISBN 978-0-600-63824-7

A CIP catalogue record for this book is available from the British Library.

Printed and bound in China.

10 9 8 7 6 5 4 3 2 1

Standard level spoon measurements are used in all recipes.
1 tablespoon = one 15 ml spoon
1 teaspoon = one 5 ml spoon
1 measure = 25 ml/1 fl oz

Both imperial and metric measurements have been given in all recipes. Use one set of measurements only and not a mixture of both.

Eggs should be medium unless otherwise stated. The Department of Health advises that eggs should not be consumed raw. This book contains dishes made with raw or lightly cooked eggs. It is prudent for more vulnerable people such as pregnant and nursing mothers, the elderly, babies and young children to avoid uncooked or lightly cooked dishes made with eggs. Once prepared these dishes should be kept refrigerated and used promptly.

Commissioning Editor: Louisa Johnson
Editor: Scarlet Furness
Recipe Editor: Laura Gladwin
Copy Editor: Harriet Webster
Editorial Assistant: Constance Lam
Creative Director: Jonathan Christie
Designer/Illustrator: Gail Guyud
Production Manager: Caroline Alberti

MIX
Paper | Supporting responsible forestry
FSC
www.fsc.org
FSC® C016973